BOSTON
OUR CITY
A View Through Children's Eyes

Sponsored by the Boston Public Library Foundation

In collaboration with Boston Public, Parochial, and Private Schools

There has been a long-standing partnership between the Boston Public Library and Boston's school systems, which has enriched the educational experience for all students. The collaborative programming which resulted in this beautiful pictorial is an example of what can be accomplished when public institutions work together for the common good. Be proud of and enjoy *Boston—Our City*!

Thomas M. Menino, Mayor of Boston

A century and more ago, through the generosity and foresight of public-spirited citizens, so much of what we value in our city was born. Whether a black minister founding a church for his people on Beacon Hill, a philanthropist and amateur musician creating what is now a world-renowned Symphony Orchestra, a Boston socialite designing a Venetian Palace in the Back Bay for her remarkable Renaissance Art Collection, or a London banker who remembered his deprived boyhood in America and helped to fund the Boston Public Library—what they and so many more accomplished long ago has not only endured, but continues to enrich all our lives and is brought to life yet again through the eyes and artwork of Boston's youth. It is the privilege of each generation not only to maintain and strengthen what has been given, but also to ensure that what was begun will continue.

Diddy Cullinane, Creator, Boston Public Library/Boston Schools Programs
Vice-Chairman, Boston Public Library Foundation

I would like to express my sincere congratulations and thanks to the Boston Public Library Foundation for their support, interest and encouragement of the children of Boston. The stimulating and exciting projects offered in this annual collaboration provide teachers with an excellent opportunity to raise awareness about the Library and the importance of books and reading. To the best of my knowledge, it is the only such successful initiative of this kind presently in existence in an urban setting. It is our hope to continue and further enhance this relationship in order to improve the quality of instruction in our schools and to provide students with lifelong interest in use of the resources of our public libraries.

Dr. Lois Harrison-Jones, Superintendent, Boston Public Schools

Contents

Cultural Institutions

Introduction

For the third year, the Boston Public Library Foundation sponsored its increasingly popular creative writing and design program in collaboration with Boston public, parochial and private schools to raise the awareness of the extraordinary community resource represented by the Boston Public Library.

In connection with the 100th Anniversary of the opening of the Library's McKim Building in Copley Square, this year's activities concentrated on the unique legacy of the City of Boston, historic and cultural, with an emphasis on events and institutions of 100 or more years ago. The historic focus was on The Freedom Trail and Black Heritage Trail, which underscore both the places and events so important to the earliest days of our city and country. Under the "umbrella" of the Boston Public Library, nine of the city's important cultural and educational organizations were represented: The Museum of Fine Arts, Boston Ballet, Gardner Museum, Museum of Afro-American History, New England Conservatory, Handel and Haydn Society, Boston Symphony Orchestra, the Science Museum, and the Boston Latin School. Because of its long-standing importance to the community, the Boston Red Sox were also included.

Thousands of students designed pictures, wrote poems, created billboards and photographed various locations within the city. Overall, 133 students were chosen to receive special recognition for their hard work and creativity. Based on grade level, the program was divided into three distinct projects:

- Elementary school students designed original drawings that represented the people, places and activities in their city. Forty-four creative designs were chosen for publication in this first-time elementary school publication *Boston—Our City*.

- More than 1,000 middle school students participated in a contest, creating original designs of Boston with captions, in either English or Spanish, for billboards placed in 200 neighborhood and school locations. Ten entries were chosen for display, including two grand-prize winners located on the Massachusetts Turnpike and Southeast Expressway for one month. An additional nine students received honorable mention, as well as fourteen submissions chosen to be published in the high school publication *Boston—Our City*, which makes for a total of thirty-three winning middle school students.

- Fifty-five high school students' essays, short stories, poems, illustrations and photographs were chosen for publication in a high school version of *Boston—Our City*.

On Saturday, May 13, 1995, the Boston Public Library Foundation held an Awards Ceremony to honor all of the participating students in this year's program. A brunch, donated by The Four Seasons Hotel, was held under a tent on the "Great Lawn" of Copley Square. Mayor Thomas M. Menino, Senate President William M. Bulger, Congressman Joseph P. Kennedy, Boston School Superintendent Lois Harrison-Jones, William O. Taylor, Chairman of the Foundation, and Diddy Cullinane, Vice Chairman of the Foundation, addressed an enthusiastic crowd of over 600 winning students, teachers, families and friends.

A special word of thanks must go out to Superintendent Lois Harrison-Jones and Foundation Vice-Chairman Diddy Cullinane who formed this beneficial collaboration back in the spring of 1992, and to Sister Ann Dominic Roach who joined in the following year. The goal of increasing the number of children utilizing the resources and services available within the Boston Public Library and its twenty-six neighborhood branches was met with overwhelming success!

Most recently, the Foundation secured funding for the "Gateway Project" coordinated by Mayor Menino and the Trustees of the Library, which connects technologically the libraries of 120 Boston public schools to the Central Library. Due to the generosity of Raytheon Corporation, the Millipore Foundation and Bank of Boston Charitable Trusts, students now have access to more than 6 million books, 1,000 periodicals and 20 government databases through their public school library as well as access to the Internet.

Foreword

It was a pleasure to be asked by the Boston Public Library Foundation and my long-time publisher and friends at Houghton Mifflin Company to write an introduction to this delightful picture book.

These beautiful pictures are done by the children of Boston. As it happens, I spent over forty years of my life in the company of a remarkable illustrator, my late husband, H. A. Rey. I understand first hand how much time, energy and love are poured into an artist's work. I see the same care and creativity in these extraordinary pictures done by the children of Boston.

I have enjoyed this tour of the city through these pictures. Now it's your turn; take your time and go slowly through these depictions by children and learn to appreciate the history and beauty Boston has to offer.

Margret Rey
Co-Author of the Curious George® *series*

Historic Sites and Events

As the birthplace of our nation, Boston has earned its title "Cradle of Liberty."

The Boston Tea Party

*The revolutionaries didn't like the taxes on tea,
so when the British ship came to port, they
dumped the tea in the Boston harbor.*

Anna Goodkind
Grade 4
Rafael Hernandez School
Roxbury
Colored marker

2

Faneuil Hall

Arlette Jacquet
Grade 4
St. Angela School
Mattapan
Colored pencil

Statue of Paul Revere in the Boston Common

Tom Bourque
Grade 4
Horace Mann School for the Deaf
Allston
Colored marker

The Boston Tea Party

Phuong Huynh
Grade 5
Franklin Roosevelt School
Hyde Park
Crayon

Boston Tea Party

***The Shirley Eustis
House, 1746***

Tom Edwards
Grade 4
Charles H. Taylor School
Mattapan
Pencil

10

The Boston Massacre

Christopher Stewart
Grade 4
East Boston Central Catholic School
East Boston
Construction paper collage with crayon

The Boston Tea Party

Alexis Hollins
Grade2
Amazing Grace Christian School
Hyde Park
Crayon

14

The U.S.S. Constitution

"Old Ironsides" with cannon balls bouncing off her hull.

Michael Dolan
Grade 1
Holy Name Parish School
West Roxbury
Crayon

16

The Old State House

Aushayla Brown
Grade 4
Charles H. Taylor School
Mattapan
Pencil

18

Churches

Joseph Creighton
Grade 3
John D. Philbrick School
Roslindale
Crayon

20

Paul Revere's Ride

John Filleti
Grade 5
Lt. J. P. Kennedy Memorial School
Hyde Park
Crayon

22

Portrait of Phillis Wheatley

Candice Baskin
Grade 2
Edward Everett School
Dorchester
Colored paper, crayon, feather, and ribbon

24

The Bunker Hill Monument

Gregory Nazzaro
Grade 5
Dennis C. Haley School
Roslindale
Crayon, pencil, and marker

26

The Old State House

Willie Brown
Grade 5
Dennis C. Haley School
Roslindale
Pencil

Old STATE House

The Boston Tea Party

Omar Fields
Grade 4
Mozart School
Roslindale
Colored marker and crayon

The Old North Church

Elizia Lopes
Grade 1
Dr. Joseph P. Tynan School
South Boston
Crayon

32

King's Chapel

Halim Lopes
Grade 4
Charles H. Taylor School
Mattapan
Pencil

34

The Old Granary Burying Ground

Jared Magee
Grade 1
Our Lady of Presentation School
Brighton
Crayon

36

The Boston Tea Party

Tainisel Rodriguez
Grade 3
Rafael Hernandez School
Roxbury
Crayon

The Soldiers and Sailors Monument in Boston Common

Duy Nguyen
Grade 4
Richard J. Murphy School
Dorchester
Crayon

40

The Old State House

Meghan Mullen
Grade 4
Margaret Fuller School
Jamaica Plain
Crayon

42

Traditional Boston Landmarks

With its beautifully designed system of parks and waterways, Boston is a delight to both children and adults.

The Swan Boats

Megan Cufaude
Grade 5
St. Mark School
Dorchester
Crayon

46

"Make Way for Ducklings"

My picture shows Mr. and Mrs. Mallard and their ducklings from the story Make Way for Ducklings *by Robert McCloskey. They are swimming in the Charles River near the Longfellow Bridge.*

Nicholas Bourne
Grade 2
Charles H. Taylor School
Mattapan
Pencil

48

Sailboats on the Charles

Jhenane Joseph
Grade 4
George H. Conley School
Roslindale
Water color

50

The Swan Boats

A swan boat travels around the lagoon at the Public Garden.

Carolyn Bird
Grade 2
St. Brendan School
Dorchester
Crayon

52

The Boston Public Garden c. 1890

Patrick Noel
Grade 5
Oliver H. Perry School
Boston
Black marker

54

Beacon Hill

Anna Santos
Grade 4
Our Lady of Presentation School
Brighton
Crayon

The Swan Boats

My picture shows the famous swan boat on the pond in the Public Garden in Boston.

Alex Magee
Grade 5
Charles H. Taylor School
Mattapan
Crayon

58

Swans

Elizabeth Lynch
Grade 2
St. Theresa School
West Roxbury
Crayon

"Make Way for Ducklings"

Paulo Barbosa
Grade 1
St. Peter School
Dorchester
Crayon

The Swan Boats Downtown

Joseph Vitiello
Grade 4
Horace Mann School for the Deaf
Allston
Colored marker

Skating in the Public Garden

Franca Edomwonyi
Grade 5
Edward Everett School
Dorchester
Colored chalk

FAO Schwarz

Marie Franzese
Grade 2
St. Mary Star of the Sea School
East Boston
Crayon

A Ride on the Swan Boats
at the Public Garden

Gabriella Ciulla
Grade 4
East Boston Central Catholic School
East Boston
Colored Marker

70

The Magical Swan Lake

Erika Nosike
Grade 5
St. Peter School
Dorchester
Crayon

The Magical Swan lake By Erika Nosike
Gr.5

Dusk at the Arboretum

Stephanie Burchett
Grade 4
George H. Conley School
Roslindale
Water color

74

Cultural Institutions

*As our country's earliest center of American culture,
Boston became known as "The Athens of America."*

Curiosity and Fascination—
Using the Science Museum

Sydney Clark
Grade 5
Joseph Lee School
Dorchester
Crayon and colored marker

The Boston Ballet

Jenette Del Monaco
Grade 5
Lt. J. P. Kennedy Memorial School
Hyde Park
Crayon

80

The Museum of Fine Arts

Sara Butterfoss
Grade 4
Margaret Fuller School
Mattapan
Crayon and colored marker

82

Happiness—Using the Library

Samantha Layne
Grade 1
Joseph Lee School
Dorchester
Crayon

84

The Boston Ballet

This is the battle between the Nutcracker and the Mouse King.

Christian Corriea
Grade 2
Oliver H. Perry School
South Boston
Colored marker

86

The Boston Pops

Jenna O'Brien
Grade 5
St. Theresa's School
West Roxbury
Crayon

The Pops

J. O'Brien

The Boston Ballet

Jennifer McGrath
Grade 4
Lt. J. P. Kennedy Memorial School
Hyde Park
Crayon

The Boston Public Library

Nicole Williams
Grade 4
St. Angela School
Mattapan
Crayon

Acknowledgments

The Boston Public Library Foundation wishes to express its gratitude to the many people who brought this volume into being.

Boston Public Schools

Dr. Lois Harrison-Jones, Superintendent.
Dr. Amanda Amis, Doreen Coyne, Martha Gillis, Albert Holland, and Dr. Dale Kalkofen.

Boston Parochial Schools

Sister Ann Dominic Roach, OP, Superintendent.
Sister Bernadette Bell, RSM, and Sister Ann Moore, CND.

Boston Public Library Trustees

Berthé M. Gaines, President.
The Honorable William M. Bulger, V. Paul Deare, Donna DePrisco, David McCullough, Pamela Seigle, Arthur F. F. Snyder, William O. Taylor, and Kim-Lan Tran.

Boston Public Library

Arthur Curley, Liam Kelly, Lesley Loke, and Jane Manthorne.

Boston Public Library Foundation Board of Directors

William O. Taylor, Agnes M. (Diddy) Cullinane, Kevin C. Phelan, Paula Alvary, Joel B. Alvord, Lawrence A. Bianchi, Arnold Bloom, Esq., Leo R. Breitman, Robin A. Brown, Stephen L. Brown, Lewis Burleigh, Esq., Marshall N. Carter, James F. Cleary, Prudence S. Crozier, John J. Cullinane, James A. Daley, Nader F. Darehshori, Lawrence S. DiCara, James S. DiStasio, Gerard F. Doherty, Esq., Ed Eskandarian, Katherine W. Fanning, Robert P. Fitzgerald, Charles Fox, Robert B. Fraser, Esq., Carol R. Goldberg, Richard Harter, Esq., Robert Haynes, Alice Hennessey, Ronald A. Homer, Jackie Jenkins-Scott, Elizabeth B. (Lillie) Johnson, Hubert E. Jones, Paul A. La Camera, Alan LeBovidge, Peter S. Lynch, Thomas J. May, Cathy E. Minehan, Paul C. O'Brien, David E. Place, Esq., Neil L. Rudenstine, Jeffrey B. Rudman, Michael Sandler, Elaine Schuster, David C. Shanks, William N. Shiebler, Susan F. Smith, Arthur F. F. Snyder, Micho F. Spring, Ira Stepanian, Jacqueline Stepanian, Earl Tate, William Van Faasen, Norman M. Wallack, Michael J. Whouley, Robert E. Wise, MD.
Staff: Karyn Wilson, Blake Jordan, and Tara Evin

Sponsors

State Street Bank, NYNEX New England, and The Birmingham Foundation.

Supporters

Jack Pow of John P. Pow Company for donating the pre-press, paper, and printing of this publication, and Robin Brown of The Four Seasons Hotel for catering the May 13, 1995, Student Awards Ceremony pro bono.

Generous Providers of Learning Materials

John Chamberlain/Globe Pequot Press for providing *The Freedom Trail*, Dan Jones/SITE Productions for creating a special version of the video *Portraits of Boston*, and Wendy Strothman/Beacon Press for supplying *Boston Sites and Insights*.

Publisher

A special thanks to Nader Darehshori, Chairman, President and Chief Executive Officer of Houghton Mifflin Company and his talented staff led by Jane Muse for editing, designing and publishing this special pictorial of *Boston—Our City*. Sarah Ambrose created the interior and cover design, Margaret Kearney provided editorial support, Dan Rademacher composed the pages, and Robin Murphy coordinated the collection of materials.